C000226740

food
eating o
second edition

Contents

food Wales
eating out guide

Published by Graffeg
Copyright © Graffeg 2010
ISBN 978 1 905582 47 1

Graffeg,
Radnor Court,
256 Cowbridge Road East,
Cardiff CF5 1GZ Wales UK.
T: +44 (0)29 2037 7312
sales@graffeg.com
www.graffeg.com

Designed and produced by
Peter Gill & Associates
sales@petergill.com
www.petergill.com

A CIP Catalogue record for this book
is available from the British Library.

Map base information reproduced
by permission of Ordnance Survey
on behalf of HMSO. © Crown
Copyright (2010). All rights
reserved. Ordnance Survey Licence
number 100020518.

Thanks to Welsh Assembly
Government Food Fisheries and
Market Development Division
for their advice, information
and support.

Food Wales eating out guide second
edition written by Colin Pressdee
with editorial research and
information from Carwyn Evans.
With thanks for assistance from our
many colleagues throughout Wales.

Every effort has been made to
ensure that the information in this
book is current and it is given in
good faith at the time of publication.
Please be aware that circumstances
can change and be sure to check
details before visiting any of the
restaurants featured.

Please note that opening times and
days might change throughout the
year with many places, particularly
in more remote areas. Always
check before setting out.

WAG FFMDD © Crown Copyright
2010. Cover: Seabass. Inside front
cover: Ultracomida, Aberystwyth;
Tyddyn Llan, Llandrillo; Slebech on
the Cleddau; Cwtch, St Davids;
The Drawing Room, Builth Wells.
Index: © Fairyhill, Reynoldston.
Inside back cover: Cwtch, St Davids;
The Ship Inn, Red Wharf Bay;
Fairyhill, Reynoldston; © Walnut
Tree, Llandewi Skirrid; Chandlery,
Newport. Back cover: Plas
Bodegroes; Tyddyn Llan, Landrillo.

How to use this guide

Places to eat are listed alphabetically A-Z in four regions of Wales – north, mid, south west and south east. Each entry in Food Wales aims to capture the general feel of the hotels, cafés and restaurants listed, providing a description of the style of the food they offer and, where applicable, giving details of their current listings in other major guides. Our price guide should be taken as a rough indication as most places offer dishes covering a broad price range. Many will also offer special set menus at lunchtime or in the early evening. Hours of opening may vary during the year, so remember to check all such details by checking individual websites or telephoning before you leave home.

Average cost of meal	£	under £20
(based on 2 courses	££	£20-30
and a glass of wine)	£££	over £30

GFG	Entry in Good Food Guide
GFG1-10	Good Food Guide rating
AA★	Automobile Association rating
	Number of beds
M★	Michelin Star
✳	Welsh Rarebits

Restaurant map location   *Restaurant contact details*   *Symbols*   *Welsh Rarebits*   *True Taste Award*

17 Crown at Whitebrook

Whitebrook, near Monmouth NP25 4TX
T: 01600 860254 www.crownatwhitebrook.co.uk
Meals £££ | GFG7 | AA★★ | 🛏 8 | M★
Manager: David Hennigan | **Chef:** James Sommerin

Dedication to culinary art and pushing boundaries of gastronomic experiences has earned a Michelin Star for five years at this secluded luxury restaurant with rooms in the lower Wye Valley ...
House specials: Braised ham hock with langoustines, celery and mustard; tortellini of butternut squash goats cheese and hazelnuts; beef sirloin with braised brisket artichokes and lentils ...

Welcome

Colin Pressdee

Since the first Food Wales eating out guide, published last autumn, there have been exciting developments in Wales. There are now four Michelin Star restaurants, from one a year ago. James Sommerin at the Crown at Whitebrook has been joined by Shaun Hill of The Walnut Tree, Shane Hughes at Ynyshir Hall and Bryan Webb of Tyddyn Llan. The publicity surrounding the Michelin Guide is excellent for attracting visitors to Wales; but there are several more restaurants that have all the makings of achieving this level of recognition.

The Welsh tradition
Chris Chown has held a Michelin Star for most of his twenty-plus years at Plas Bodegroes. Mary Ann Gilchrist of Carlton Riverside held a star for several years for cooking with great flair. There are many restaurants that have been highly rated in the Good Food Guide for well over a decade. One is Ye Olde Bull's Head Loft Restaurant, due to the hard work of long time owners Keith Rothwell and David Robertson. Similarly Peter and Janet Pitman's beautiful boutique Tan-Y-Foel has been top rated with highly inspiring cuisine. Fairyhill has long upheld high standards and continues breaking culinary ground using local food from Gower.

Top rated restaurants
I consider there are at least twenty restaurants with highly capable chefs who use best locally sourced seasonal food. Gareth Johns, the Wynnstay;

Glyn Roberts, the Castle Cottage; Susannah Woods of Neuadd Lwyd; Huw and Beth Roberts, Gwesty Cymru; Ian Bennet, the Welcome to Town; Peter Jackson, Maes y Neuadd; Graham Tinsley, the Castle Conwy; Stephen Terry, the Hardwick; Simon King, 1861, and Matt Tebbutt at the Foxhunter are some in this league. Others have top cuisine in a distinctive ambience, such as: the Harbourmaster, the Falcondale, Le Gallois, Porth Tocyn, the West Arms, Llys Meddyg, Cnapan, the Bell, the Bear, and the Felin Fach Griffin. Many of these have been recipients of True Taste Awards.

Some great little places

Welsh Rarebits, the unique hotel group, has for over twenty five years selected places that have maintained impeccable standards of Welsh hospitality. The welcome, comforts, facilities, ambience and cuisine are all part of the experience. With over fifty members they are all individual, distinctive, mostly owner run and many have chef patrons. They are located throughout Wales and offer true Welsh hospitality.

There are an increasing number of chef/patron restaurants that show flair with local seasonal produce such as Illtyd's, Bwyty Mawddach, Slice and the Ship Inn, Red Wharf Bay. It's also good to see genuine pubs that offer fine food retaining a local ambience. The Old Kings Arms, The Queen's Head, The King Arthur and The Angel Hotel in Abergavenny are great examples. Many cafés have impeccable simpler locally sourced food such as Town Hall and Blue Sky.

It has been encouraging to see continued investment in catering, with many places being revamped and brought into the 21st century including the Fountain, Traeth, the New Conway and the Royal Oak.

In the new guide I trust you will find places with good food at all levels, from the Michelin Stars to the many smaller local places.

I hope you will enjoy eating out in Wales in the coming year.

Recommendations

If you wish to comment on places listed or not listed in this book, please fill out the comment form at www.graffeg.com and email to foodwales@graffeg.com

Assessing restaurants

Contemporary Wales offers a wide choice of restaurants of contrasting styles. Most hotels boast restaurants open to non-residents, and the number of pubs, cafés and wine bars selling meals has also been bolstered. These businesses are run by a mix of people, and very few of them entered the industry as their original chosen career.

The most interesting places to eat are owned by individuals or families who in some way put a personal stamp on their food style, service and décor. Therefore this guide has chosen to overlook the more formulaic urban chain restaurants which sell burgers, pasta or pizza.

It takes great organisational skill to run a good restaurant. It is quite unlike catering at home for a dinner party, because most customers are initially unknown to you, and people have widely differing expectations.

The skills needed to run a kitchen and the front of house are equally important, and each depends on the other. The modern style of restaurant, with an open kitchen visible from the restaurant, has brought the two closer together. Many chefs who worked in old-fashioned, large hotels never saw the restaurant, let alone its customers.

Culinary techniques

The cooking skills required depend on the type of restaurant and the range of cuisine served. It may sound obvious to some but a chef in a steakhouse needs to know how to grill meat. A top kitchen might employ several culinary techniques and use a wide range of meat, fish, vegetables, dairy and bakery produce. And so the arts of baking, frying, grilling, poaching, roasting, making sauces and pastry, together with food presentation must all be understood.

The chef and his team must know the quality and provenance of their ingredients, and where to source them. It pays to build a rapport with suppliers because although there are many sound suppliers in Wales, getting a delivery can still be a problem in some remote areas.

A restaurateur has to know the style of food on offer on any given menu. The more complex the menu, and the broader the

choice, the more resources are required.

The style of service must be in keeping with the menu and the style of the restaurant. Front of house staff work on the front line, giving the customer his or her first impression of an establishment. Their social skills set the tone from the reception to the bar and restaurant. Each member of a good team will be able to anticipate the needs of every customer and provide unobtrusive service. Knowledge of the menu, of the origins of the dishes and their ingredients, and a seamless wine service complement the quality of the food on offer.

For most catering operations the overall cost of the staff is the biggest outlay. In Wales, as everywhere else, expensive restaurants delivering fine food and service can represent good value. On the other hand, some less expensive places seriously under-deliver and are very poor value.

Top recommendations

I have been writing about restaurants in Wales since the 1980s in many publications including the Western Mail,

Wales on Sunday, and Financial Times. We produced Dining Out in Wales in 2004, Food Wales in 2005 and Food Wales – a second helping in 2008. Over the years I have visited most corners of Wales and eaten in many restaurants, pubs, cafés and tea rooms. Many of the owners and staff I know personally.

This guide is derived from this experience. I also know many people who eat out regularly in Wales and rely on a large number of contacts who know their region well, and who feed back information on new and established eateries.

The information presented in this guide cross refers with other major guides including The Good Food Guide, The AA Restaurant Guide, The Michelin Guide, Welsh Rarebits and others. Entries are placed into two main categories. Short entries might be attractive, particularly in more remote places, or have a fair offer for price, though some might vary in reliability. Longer entries might be listed as top recommendations: the very finest places to eat in Wales.

Welsh food

Wales produces a remarkable variety of food for such a small country. Welsh lamb is the best known product, with farms across the nation rearing flocks. From early spring to late autumn lamb is plentiful and varies in flavour as the seasons progress. As the grazing varies from the crags of Cadair Idris to the salt marshes of the Mawddach, the rolling pastures of Radnorshire, or the expansive moorlands of Llanbrynmair or Llandegla, so does the taste and flavour. All Welsh lamb has a Protected Geographical Indication (PGI) which provides the catering industry and its customers with an assurance of quality.

Cattle are reared for both dairy produce and meat in most areas. Small farms might specialise in traditional Welsh Black beef, although most stock other well-known breeds. An increasing amount is produced organically, adding to the choice of quality.

It is great to see a growing interest in traditional breeds of pig on Welsh farms, including the Welsh breed, the Saddleback and the Old Spot. These are particularly attractive to specialist restaurants and retailers. Free range poultry fits into the same type of traditional mixed farming and is similarly popular.

Wild game

There is an abundance of reared and wild game throughout Wales, particularly pheasant and deer on the great estates. There is also much to attract the forager who through the seasons can find plenty of wild mushrooms, berries, plants and nuts. These characters usually have friendly connections with local restaurants and hotels.

Fish and shellfish

The Welsh coastline yields a bounty of produce, particularly where it has been fished in a sustainable way. The mussel fishery at Bangor on the Menai Straits is a classic example of good husbandry and stable, healthy stocks. The nation's inshore fishery in general is considered to be in a healthy state. The establishment of marine conservation areas such as Lundy Island is already having a beneficial effect on stocks in surrounding waters, and more of these will further boost stocks.

The number of shellfisheries for crab and lobster has remained stable while an increase in local processing, particularly of crab, has protected its added value. Harvests of the main fish species for the catering industry, particularly bass, remain healthy. Other species such as sole, plaice, turbot, skate, cod, mackerel, monk and mullet are landed by inshore trawlers but most, including shellfish, now go directly to foreign markets. The supply of local seafood to inland restaurants is difficult in most areas of Wales. And as inshore fisheries are highly weather-dependent supplies can be erratic.

Declining natural runs of wild salmon and sewin in Welsh rivers is of concern to conservationists and anglers, as well as to caterers. In most places supplies of farmed salmon and sea trout have replaced the wild on menus.

Farmhouse cheese
Wales' dairy industry, particularly its organic sector and cheese producers, is very successful. Farming co-operatives provide fresh milk, cream, butter and cheese on a large scale. Rachel's Dairy has been the pioneering organic brand that has encouraged many others to follow suit. Artisan and farmhouse cheese producers now supply a range of different types of cheese that are widely available to the catering industry via some of the well- known produce wholesalers, such as Castell Howell, Vin Sullivan and Caws Cymru.

Vegetables
Seasonal vegetables, such as Pembroke and Gower new potatoes, cauliflowers, leeks, cabbages and roots, and more specialist produce, such as salad goods and asparagus, are available in season, some in very good quantity.

Specialist food and drink
More and more specialist food manufacturers are producing charcuterie, such as pâtés, cured and smoked meat and fish, and organic sea salt and bakery products. Similarly, the number of independent breweries in Wales has swollen to over forty, supplying a wide range of popular traditional ales. Many Welsh vineyards are reaching maturity and are producing very acceptable light styles of white, red and sparkling wines. Country wine and spirit producers also find a popular local market for their drinks. Penderyn single malt whisky is almost obligatory on the back counters of bars in Wales' restaurants, hotels and gastropubs now it has been praised for its quality by Britain's leading whisky experts.

something for everyone

Whether you want to mark a special occasion by dining in style, a relaxed family meal, or the occasional treat, Wales has something for everyone – from Michelin Star restaurants and hotels to cafés and tearooms. Wales has a thriving food scene, with an increasing number of chefs and cooks taking advantage of the wealth of superb produce on offer.

Indeed, the Eating Out section forms an important part of the annual Wales the True Taste Food and Drink Awards, the keenly contested categories illustrating the talent and passion for food which exists in Wales.

For nearly ten years the Wales the True Taste brand has been the standard bearer for the Welsh food and drink industry, catching the imagination of consumers and food and drink industry insiders alike who regard it as a mark of quality and excellence.

The brand has a new look, the refreshed logo connecting with and sharing the values of the Welsh Assembly Government's vision for Wales as a whole, and re-enforcing Wales' reputation for flavoursome and innovative cuisine.

Says Rural Affairs Minister, Elin Jones: *"The True Taste brand which has been refreshed this year aims to promote the very best of what our country has to offer. In Wales we see food and drink as a great adventure, something to feed the imagination as well as the appetite. We're proud of our food and the people who make it."*

The 2010 True Taste Awards ceremony is to be held at Pembrokeshire's County Showground as part of the Welsh Assembly Government's strategy to take the awards closer to the people of Wales; in 2011 the venue will be in North Wales, and the new Food Hall at the Royal Welsh Showground in Llanelwedd in 2012.

For more information about the Wales the True Taste Food & Drink Awards please log on to:

www.truetaste.tv / www.gwirflas.tv

For more information about Welsh food and drink log on to:

www.walesthetruetaste.co.uk

Cwtch

It is Wales' most westerly town and Britain's smallest city, and now St David's is home to one of the rising stars of the Welsh hospitality scene – Cwtch.

Run by owner Rachael Knott and head chef Matt Cox, the 50 seat restaurant takes its name from the Welsh term for 'hug', and certainly its interior with slate floors, chalk boards and comfy seating creates a warm and welcoming environment.

It was the combination of ambience and good food which won Cwtch the West Wales title in the restaurant category of the 2009 True Taste Awards.

"The food we can source locally is simply amazing," says Rachael. "The crab from Abercastle is so good and Springfield Farm at Manorbier gets us wonderful asparagus."

Indeed the restaurant is featured in the Michelin Red Guide, and also covered in the Good Food Guide, and uses local ingredients to flavoursome effect.

The result is a menu filled with dishes like Slow Roasted Pork Belly with Black Pudding, Apple Sauce & Onion Gravy; Stuffed Portobello Mushrooms, Pantysgawn Goats Cheese with Spiced Aubergines & Puy Lentils; and Dark Chocolate Pot with Merlyn Liqueur Cream Shot & Flapjack.

The AA guide-listed restaurant is very much at the heart of the community, sourcing locally produced ingredients and regularly holding public events.

Also, when he's not creating culinary masterpieces in the kitchen Matt turns his hand to saving lives as a member of the St David's RNLI lifeboat team.

www.cwtchrestaurant.co.uk (page entry 82).

Tyddyn Llan

Nestling in the peaceful Vale of Edeyrnion is the epitome of culinary delight and relaxation – Tyddyn Llan Restaurant with Rooms.

The elegant Georgian house in Llandrillo on the eastern fringes of the Snowdonia National Park has been transformed into a Michelin Star gastronomic haven by husband and wife team Bryan and Susan Webb.

After several years running a restaurant in London's Kensington, Pontypool born chef Bryan returned to his Welsh roots when he and Susan took over Tyddyn Llan in 2002.

The accolades keep on coming too and the True Taste Award-winning restaurant is the highest rated Welsh establishment in the current Good Food Guide and is also the guide's 2010 Readers Restaurant of the Year.

It is renowned for using a variety of local and Welsh produce to create innovative and flavoursome food, something which is becoming increasingly important to consumers too.

Bryan and Susan use the best seasonal produce from a network of local suppliers, such as Organic Pork from Llanuwchllyn is used to create Fillet, Belly with Black Pudding, Braised Cheek and Breaded Trotter with Shallot and Thyme Puree. The catch from Cardigan Bay becomes the mouthwatering Dressed Crab with Melon, Wet Almonds and Fennel.

Says Bryan, "We use some fantastic Welsh lamb, beef and pork, chicken and duck – indeed 75% of the food we serve is sourced locally, we use as much Welsh produce as possible. If the local food is good then people should buy it because it keeps the local butcher and farmer in business, it helps everyone."

www.tyddynllan.co.uk (page entry 52).

Pannacotta

By Bryan Webb, Chef Proprietor, Tyddyn Llan

Serves 6

Ingredients

150g	caster sugar	3	leaves of gelatine
600ml	double cream	2	tbsp Celtic Spirit Company's Black Mountain Liqueur
150ml	milk		
2	vanilla pods (optional) split in two lengthways	4 to 5	blood oranges segmented

Method

Put the cream, milk and vanilla pod into a large saucepan and slowly bring to the boil. Lower the heat and leave to simmer for 5 minutes.

Meanwhile put the gelatine into cold water to soften, then drain off all the water.

Stir in the sugar and Black Mountain Liqueur, allow to dissolve, remove from the heat and slip in the softened gelatine. Stir well and strain through a fine sieve, leave to cool and stir from time to time.

Place 6 dariole moulds, small soup bowls or glass dishes on a tray and pour the cold cream into the moulds. Refrigerate until set.

To serve run a small knife around the moulds, place in a bowl of boiling hot water for 10 seconds, turn onto a cold plate and wait for it to go 'plop' out of the mould, it should be very delicate and wobbly. Place the orange segments around and drizzle with a little extra liqueur.

The Crown at Whitebrook

It may be tucked away in a wooded valley but the Crown at Whitebrook is at the summit of the Welsh culinary scene.

For the past four years the restaurant at Whitebrook, near Monmouth, has been the recipient of a Michelin Star, and was for some time Wales' only Michelin restaurant.

Together, Executive Head Chef James Sommerin and General Manager David Hennigan have created an award-winning team, with David named 2010 Restaurant Manager of the Year by the Academy of Food and Wine Service.

"It was an honour to have been a standard bearer and the only restaurant with a Michelin Star in Wales but I am thrilled that we've now been joined by three other restaurants each with their own single star," says Executive Head Chef James Sommerin, who also heads The Crown at Celtic Manor restaurant, awarded 3 AA rosettes.

"There are some amazing producers and produce in Wales and the Michelin Stars will help further showcase the country as a food destination."

Much of the ingredients are sourced from the surrounding area, where there is a 'reservoir' of fellow True Taste Award winners such as Raglan Butcher, NS James – where the meat can be traced to individual animals – and ewe's milk cheese producer Caws Mynydd Ddu from Talgarth, while the county's fields and the foreshore are foraged for ingredients.

The result is a mouthwatering menu including dishes like Welsh Venison Loin with Spiced Carrot, Coffee, Sorrel and Wild mushroom; Smoked Lamb, Braised neck, Rosemary, Celeriac, Tomato, and the delectable Apricot with Hazelnut, Dark Chocolate and Salted Caramel.

www.crownatwhitebrook.co.uk (page entry 108).

Welsh lamb with wild rice, squid and ras al hanout

By James Sommerin, Executive Head Chef, the Crown at Whitebrook

Serves 4

Ingredients

4 x 150g	Welsh lamb loin		3	red peppers skinned and deseeded
4	baby squid		1	sprig rosemary
50g	wild rice		100g	butter
½	onion		1tsp	Ras al Hanout
1	sprig rosemary		250ml	dark meat stock
½	red pepper skinned and deseeded		100ml	red wine
300ml	chicken stock		100ml	Port
100g	butter			

Method

Wild rice

Finely chop and sauté the onion and pepper, add the wild rice, rosemary and 225ml of the stock. Cook at 160°C in a pre heated oven until the rice becomes soft. Add the remaining chicken stock, return to the oven checking regularly until thick.

Pepper puree

Skin, deseed and quarter the peppers. Place into a pan with the butter and rosemary and warm gently for 1 hour – the butter should not take on any colour.

Drain off the butter and remove the rosemary, blend the peppers until smooth using a hand blender/liquidiser and season to taste.

Sauce

Boil together the Port, red wine and Ras al Hanout until reduced by half. Add the stock and reduce by half again.

Lamb

Sear the lamb in a hot pan for 3-5 minutes either side. Remove to a plate and rest for 5 minutes.

The baby squid should also be seared in a hot pan for no longer than 30 seconds.

The Walnut Tree

A pivotal part of Monmouthshire's culinary reputation, The Walnut Tree at Llanddewi Skirrid was awarded its Michelin Star at the beginning of 2010.

Shaun Hill and William Griffiths took over The Walnut Tree in December 2007, after moving across the border from gourmet destination Ludlow where Shaun's restaurant, The Merchant House, was the first in the town to win a Michelin Star.

A desire for larger premises, coupled with the availability of excellent local produce, brought him to Abergavenny and an area with impeccable foodie credentials – Monmouthshire won the inaugural True Taste Food Tourism Destination award in 2008 and is bursting with food of the highest quality.

This is reflected in The Walnut Tree's exciting menu which is based on chef Shaun's personal taste and sound cooking techniques which have been honed to perfection over 40 years in the culinary world.

These are fused together with a basis of excellent ingredients to create delectable dishes like Roast Wood Pigeon with Morel & Sweetbread Sausage; Sirloin of Beef with Potato Gnocchi & Salsa Verde, and the tantalizing Gingered Nectarine & Blueberry Pudding.

"I am building up a group of all-year-round local suppliers," *says Shaun.*

"If you are working with rather ordinary ingredients it takes a lot of effort and fancy footwork to make something good out of it. But if the produce is good you are half-way there."

This is in tune with increasing consumer interest in the origins of the food on their plates. Says Shaun, *"People are more interested in produce; they care about its provenance – the way meat is produced – and sustainability of commodities like fish."*

www.thewalnuttreeinn.com (page entry 118).

Twice baked goat's cheese soufflé

By Shaun Hill, Chef Proprietor of The Walnut Tree

Serves 4

Ingredients

125ml	whole milk	125g	fresh Pant-y-Sgawn goats cheese – crumbled
25g	unsalted butter		
25g	plain flour		
2	egg yolks	1tsp	English mustard
3	egg whites – whisked until stiff	1tsp	Worcestershire sauce
1tsp	cornflour	Dash of Tabasco sauce
		Salt and pepper	

Method

Pre-heat the oven to 180°C. Heat the milk.

Melt the butter in a large saucepan. Add the flour and stir to a smooth glossy paste. Cook for 2 minutes. Add the hot milk, whisking all the time until the sauce is thick.

Remove from the heat then beat in the egg yolks and cornflour. Fold in the egg white then all the other ingredients.

Spoon the mixture into 4-5 greased ramekins. Place into a deep roasting tray. Fill to halfway with water then bake in the pre-heated oven until risen – about 15 minutes. Remove from the roasting tray and allow to cool.

To serve, run a small palette knife around the edge of the ramekin and carefully turn out the soufflés. Place them the right way up on a baking tray. Bake at 180°C for 10 –15 minutes until golden and puffed.

Ynyshir Hall Hotel

It is the synchronicity of solitude and luxury which make a stay at Ynyshir Hall at Eglwysfach, near Machynlleth such a memorable experience. Once owned by Queen Victoria, Ynyshir Hall is set in 14 acres of superb grounds amidst the Dyfi Estuary. The sourcing of local produce is central to the ethos of the hotel's 3 AA rosette and True Taste Award-winning restaurant, which was awarded a Michelin Star in 2010.

The fruits of the surrounding hills and nearby coast are used to spectacular effect by head chef Shane Hughes to create fabulous fare, such as Dyfi Estuary Sea Trout with Wild Garlic Gnocchi, Aubergine, Fennel & Wood Sorrel; Local Organic Pork tenderloin with Crab & Spring Onion Tortellini and Spiced Honey & Ginger Cappuccino; and Assiette of Welsh Black Beef: Fillet, Sweetbread, Shin Ravioli & Samosa enhanced with Asian Spices.

Shane uses wild foods which he acquires from the local area and he invites guests to join him in discovering items like wild samphire and wild garlic for use in the kitchen.

Says Shane, *"Since moving to Wales four years ago I have been impressed with the enthusiasm of the people around Powys and Ceredigion to promote and sell their goods.*

"Obviously it is in their interest, but also there seems to be a passion seldom seen in other areas of the UK where quality product often simply means high prices.

"In return I have done my utmost to champion the Welsh food and sing its praises at every opportunity.

"All this, of course, is for a reason, the sweetest and most tender lobsters, the most succulent pork, delicious beef and of course the lamb speaks for itself. With this in mind I shall continue to enjoy the Welsh larder."

www.ynyshirhall.co.uk (page entry 75).

Brined and braised Welsh pork

By Shane Hughes, Head Chef, Ynyshir Hall Hotel

Serves 6

Preparation time: 3 days
(brine for at least 24 hours for
maximum flavour)

Cooking time: 3 hours

Ingredients

6	pigs' cheeks	10	cloves
2	pigs' tongues	5	star anise
1	pork belly	4	bay leaves
4	bottles of SA Gold Welsh Beer	6	sprigs of thyme
500	salt	400ml	white wine
250g	each of chopped onion, carrot, celery & leek	400ml	red wine
		250ml	sherry vinegar
5	cloves garlic	200ml	clear honey
10g	coriander seeds	3ltr	chicken stock
		150ml	olive oil

Method

Stage 1

Skin the pork belly and remove any bones.

Roll the pigs' cheeks and tongues in pork belly and tie firmly with butcher's string.

Boil the salt and ale together. Allow to cool. Marinade the pork in salt/ale brine for 24 hours.

Stage 2

Pre-heat the heavy bottom saucepan and sauté the vegetables and garlic until golden brown. Pour in sherry vinegar, honey, thyme, bay leaf, star anise, coriander seeds and cloves and reduce by two thirds.

Add white and red wine and reduce by half. Add chicken stock.

Remove the pork from brine, wash lightly and dry thoroughly.

Sauté the pork belly in olive oil until deep golden brown, add to stock and bring to simmer.

Foil the pan then put a lid on. Cook in the oven gas mark 3/150 degrees C for 3 hours.

Remove from the oven and allow to cool entirely in the stock.

Remove from the stock and pass juice through sieve and reduce while skimming until required consistency.

Cut the string off the pork and serve with sauce and vegetables.

WELSH RAREBITS®
Hotels of Distinction

Welsh Rarebits is a portfolio of over fifty hotels. This unique collection of hotels is actually more of a coterie than any other group. Each one has been hand picked for the ethos of extending a warm welcome and genuine Welsh hospitality; each in its own way is special. Many are owner run and with a chef/patron. Perhaps the fifth brochure, over twenty years ago, personified the individuality of Welsh Rarebits places as the hotel featured on the cover was Tyddyn Llan which this year gained a coveted Michelin Star for its superb cuisine.

Growing in size

From then the coterie has grown from twenty six hotels to over fifty, yet ten of the originals are still members and are run by the same people. These places have retained the indefinable sense of atmosphere and character that comes from personal service and an attention to detail at every level. The forty plus places that have joined since those days have kept the imagination alive, and brought creativity and broader character to the group. The choice has now blossomed to include boldly contemporary townhouses, new and high end seaside hotels, chic country inns, state-of-the-art spas and famous foodie restaurants with rooms.

What makes each place individual is a combination of intricate factors. The central ethos throughout contributes to the character of each. Many are renowned for their cuisine; some have stunning architecture and interior design; locations vary from the centre of towns to remote countryside; handsome state of the art leisure facilities and spas might be a main attraction and perhaps stunning grounds and gardens; the ambience of a genuine local pub without the tat of the ubiquitous chain public houses might be a kindling part of the ambience of significant catering operations.

Ambience

The Bear Hotel in Crickhowell has a bar that is still the hub of the local community. Perhaps the same can be said of the Beaufort, the Hand and the Felin Fach Griffin. These also have superb food, accommodation and ambience. Some have developed more into pub-restaurants, while retaining a local feel, such as at

Felin Fach Griffin, Brecon.

Cleifiog Uchaf, and Llanwenarth Arms which also have fine rural locations as an added attraction.

Beautiful locations

Perhaps the location is all; Hotel Portmeirion, set on the waterfront of the Italianate village; The Harbourmaster on the quay has the finest views over Cardigan Bay where much of the food served comes from. Similarly Ty'n Rhos surveys the Menai, Anglesey and Snowdonia for culinary inspiration of the fabulous rural settings of Llansantffraed Court, Crug Glas, Warpool Court and Slebech give an air of supreme spaciousness. The glorious and discreet locations of Jabajak, the Grove and Pen-y-Dyffryn set the tone for the treats inside.

The striking Victorian architecture of Miskin Manor, the amazing Norman folly of Castell Deudraeth and the elegant Italianate Falcondale certainly show no two places are alike, yet this personifies their individuality. The glorious rural architecture of Llys Meddyg, Penally Abbey and the grand Manorhaus not surprisingly have something in common, which is real Welsh hospitality inside.

Food Wales eating out guide – second edition

Relaxation ✳

Many tourists now look for the relaxing pleasures of the mind, body and soul. Spa holidays are an important and growing sector of tourism in every beautiful country. Many of the hotels have leisure facilities, some with magnificent suites and spas. Businessmen and tourists relax in the leisure suites of Coed-y-Mwstwr, Lamphey Court, Lake Vyrnwy, and the Penrallt. Finest spa facilities and treatments are part of the broad offering of St. Brides, The Lake and Bodysgallen Hall.

Business or leisure? ✳

The location of many urban and rural hotels is convenient for both leisure and business visitors. On the borderland Milebrook House, The Royal Oak, Pen-y-Dyffryn and Northop Hall serve as the heralds for incoming tourists to experience Welsh hospitality. Beautifully located in the North Wales countryside and coastline are Pentre Mawr, Sychnant Pass and Rhiwafallen. Some are in delightful village locations in South Wales such as the remote Ty Mawr, the western Wolfscastle and the Great House in the Vale of Glamorgan.

Welsh food ✳

Good quality, locally sourced and seasonal food is part of the offering of real Welsh hospitality. The great houses of Wales have been renowned for their fine tables since the middle ages when travelling bards added the entertainment. Every member establishment offers the fine fare of the area and many have been recognised for their cuisine for decades particularly in North Wales. Of the original members Ye Olde Bull's Head, Maes Y Neuadd, Tyddyn Llan and Fairyhill are still among the top places in Britain in the major food guides. Long established are Tan-Y-Foel, St Tudno, Penmaenuchaf Hall, the Castle, Peterstone Court and the Crown at Whitebrook. Fabulous newer places are Neuadd Llwyd and Gwesty Cymru.

Wales, for a relatively small country, probably produces a wider range of food from the land and sea than almost any other country. As the seasons unfold, the produce available gives endless inspiration to chefs and Wales does have some of the leading chefs in Britain. There are now four Michelin Star chefs in Wales, two of them current Welsh Rarebits members. Bryan Webb at Tyddyn Llan and James Sommerin of the Crown at Whitebrook both produce outstanding cuisine although they are quite different and individual in style. There are many of the hotel chefs who are in the top league producing great cuisine from locally sourced seasonal ingredients, and this is an important part of Welsh hospitality.

Penmaenuchaf Hall Hotel, Penmaenpool.

The Welsh Rarebits website: **www.rarebits.co.uk** gives all the information on members of the coterie and will guide you through making any arrangements.

Book online
All places can be booked online, and there is lots of information on Special Offers, best prices and unique possibilities.

Loyalty card & brochure
The Welsh Rarebits loyalty card gives extra special treatment offerings, special rates and promotions. A brochure can be requested online: this is an essential accompaniment when travelling into Wales.

Gift voucher
For a novel Christmas or birthday present Welsh Rarebits Gift Vouchers invite friends and family to share the experience.

Welsh Rarebits Prince's Square, Montgomery SY15 6PZ, Wales, UK. Tel: 01686 668030 email: info@rarebits.co.uk
www.rarebits.co.uk

Welsh Independent Brewers

In the past decade the Welsh brewing industry has blossomed and there are now over forty breweries within Wales. In size they vary from the giants such as S.A. Brain of Cardiff and Hurns Brewery in Swansea, down to the more boutique breweries such as Purple Moose Brewery of Porthmadog, Penlon Cottage Brewery, the Breconshire Brewery, Otley Brewing Company of Pontypridd, Monty's Brewery, Montgomery, and The Celt Experience of Caerphilly. The smaller breweries are spread all over the country and there is hardly an area that doesn't have a local brewery. From Flint to Conwy, Snowdon to Ceredigion, Dowlais to Bishopston, Llanrwst to Lampeter there are local ales to be found in a broad number of shops, pubs, hotels and restaurants.

Brewing skills

Brewing is as much of an art as wine making. There has to be a balance of the ingredients and method that will make up exactly what the brewer is looking for. Malted barley, hops, yeast and water are the ingredients for beer and it is amazing how these can be turned into a wide range of styles according to each individual recipe used. The style can be from a light and zesty lager through to a full weighty stout, so there are numerous possibilities for matching some fine Welsh local food to the local ales.

Beer and food combinations

Matching food with beer is not for the cheap end of the market. The top restaurant in London, the long established Le Gavroche in Mayfair, has a beer list that is presented with their wine list. Chef Michel Roux Jnr personally selects the beers for the list to match his grand cuisine. His impeccable food ranges from light shellfish dishes through to the greatest bastions of French traditional gastronomy such as braised oxtail and jarret of beef. The range of Welsh produce available to the restaurants listed in this guide gives a complete menu choice covering everything from the land and sea. Mussels, oysters, scallops, crab, lobster, bass, sewin, sole, plaice and cod are some of the most popular seafood on menus, while Welsh lamb and beef, specialist breeds of pork, poultry, and game make a varied choice of

ADVERTORIAL

Otley Brewing Company; Monty's Brewery.

meats throughout the seasons. The dairy industry provides a wide range of cheeses from traditional block cheddars through to the craft cheeses from cows, goats and sheep milk.

Selecting a beer to go with a meal is much the same as selecting wine. The weight of the beer should match the power of the food. Just as a Muscadet is perfect with shellfish, so a crisp lager or IPA will go equally well. A ragout of lamb with its sweet herb nuances will go with beer that has a richer complexity. A heavy casserole of beef will match nicely with a deeper flavoured beer such as a porter or stout.

Matching cheese with beer is one of the real delights because the style of cheese can vary from an astringent goats cheese through to a creamy soft brie style or a full mature cheddar, Caerphilly or a rich blue cheese. The matching beer can be something flowery and dry through to rich and sweet, each finding its level and partner on the table.

A wide range of flavours

The joy of the independent brewers is that each makes a range of styles of beers to give variety and choice. The days of mild or bitter are long over, for the craft of the brewer comes through in the range that they can make from the four basic ingredients. The malting of the grain, the variety of hop and how they are infused plus the fermentation from the yeast gives an almost infinite number of possible ales. Finding the range that will be popular and profitable is the art.

Welsh brewers

The **Breconshire Brewery** has a range of Contemporary and Traditional Cask and Bottle Conditioned Beers, all drawing influence and names from the locality. All the beers have been designed to be enjoyed on their own, or with the fabulous local produce – try Red Dragon with pheasant or other game,

Ramblers Ruin with Welsh Black Beef or Cribyn with fresh caught trout.

The Otley Brewery has the range of styles called O1, O2, O3 etc which gives an indication of the weight of each. The concept is easy to understand and match against the weight of the food.

The Celt Experience makes a wonderful true lager that is well-aged to develop its lightness and elegant complexity and hence this is a great match for a wide range of seafood and light meat dishes. Their Bronze and Gold as the name suggests are the deeper and more weighty ales that go very well with meat dishes and many of the Welsh farmhouse cheeses.

Purple Moose has a range of ales that will match the diversity of the food from the freshest Aberdaron lobster through to Menai mussels and mountain lamb.

Monty's in the rural border land has some signature accounts that sell a range of their beers, matched so well to the rich meat and dairy produce of the region.

What next for Welsh brewing?

Now that many of the pubs throughout Wales have elevated their catering as listed through the regions, so have they increased their range of local ales. The brewing industry in Wales is something for all to be proud of and the partnership between the vibrant Welsh food industry and Welsh brewing should be nurtured at all levels. It will be good to see many of the top restaurants in Wales following Michel Roux Jnr's lead and produce lists of local ales to match their renowned cuisine.

The Association of Welsh Independent Brewers

The Association was set up in 2008 to help improve sales and opportunities through marketing, quality promotion and emphasis of the Welsh identity for Wales' Brewing Industry Since the turn of the Millennium, the number of breweries in Wales has increased dramatically, along with the quality and diversity of locally produced beers. The public perception of local produce as quality produce has also seen demand develop. However, Wales is not yet regarded as one of the finest brewing nations, something the Association intends to change. In past years, Welsh brewers have won awards for their beers both on a national (UK) scale, including 4 medals in the 2010 CAMRA Champion Beer of Britain Awards, and internationally, including 3 medals at the International Beer Challenge. AWIB aims to

Celt Experience, Bronze Crafted Ale; Breconshire Brewery Ales.

develop the public perception of Wales as a place where local producers create some of the world's finest drink and food. This astonishing array of flavours that Wales' food and drink producers create can stand alone, but also work together to compliment and contrast each other for a truly remarkable experience.

Welsh Independent Brewers
Please visit **www.awib.org.uk** for more information.

- Artisan, Cardiff
- Breconshire, Brecon
- Bryncelyn, Ystradgynlais
- Bullmastiff, Cardiff
- Celt Experience, Caerphilly
- Cerddyn, Maesteg
- Conwy, Conway
- Facers, Flint
- Felinfoel, Llanelli
- Great Orme, Glan Conwy
- Gwaun Valley, Fishgaurd
- Hay, Hay-on-Wye
- Jacobi, Caio
- Jolly Brewer, Wrexham
- Kingstone, Tintern
- Heart of Wales, Llanwrtyd Wells
- McGivern's Ales, Wrexham
- Monty's, Montgomery

- Nant, Llanrwst
- North Wales, Abergele
- Otley, Pontypridd
- Pen-Lon Cottage, Llanarth
- Plassey, Wrexham
- Preselli Brewery, Tenby
- Purple Moose, Porthmadog
- Rhymney, Merthyr Tydfil
- Rotters, Talgarth
- S.A. Brain, Cardiff
- Sandstone, Wrexham
- Snowdonia, Waunfawr
- Swansea, Bishopston
- Tomos Watkin, Swansea
- Tudor, Abergavenny
- Vale of Glamorgan, Barry
- Warcop, Newport
- Waen, Newtown

North Wales: where to eat

Here is some of the most dramatic 'Wild Wales' scenery in Britain. Set in this beautiful landscape are impressive country house hotels with timeless reputations for fine cuisine. Michelin Star Tyddyn Llan, the majestic Plas Bodegroes, the hidden retreats of Tan-Y-Foel at Capel Garmon, Maes y Neuadd, Talsarnau, Castle Cottage Harlech and the old coaching hotel Ye Olde Bulls Head in Beaumaris are all highly acclaimed. Numerous smaller restaurants and boutique hotels make this area an excellent destination.

It is under three hours from Birmingham to Anglesey or Aberdaron, and less than two from Chester. The accessibility of the Snowdonia National Park, or the rugged Llŷn Peninsula opens up numerous tourist facilities. Sailing, fishing, swimming, walking, climbing and eating can all be part of a day out. Nowhere is there such a selection of natural food: Conwy mussels; Aberdaron crab and lobster; mountain lamb from Snowdonia, or from the Mawddach salt marshes, plus wonderful beer from many small breweries.

Opposite: Glyn Roberts, Castle Cottage, Harlech; Tyddyn Llan, Llandrillo.

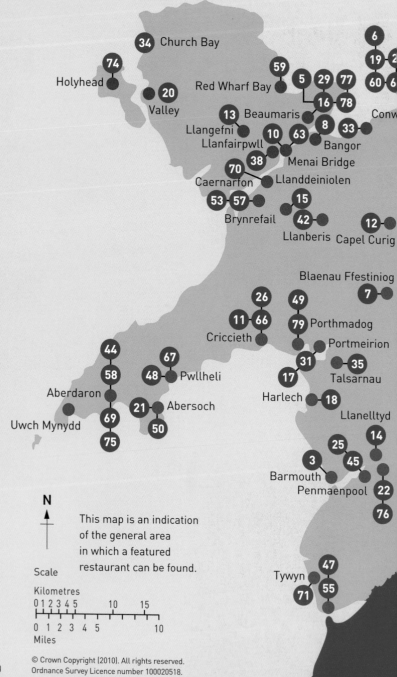

34 Church Bay

74 Holyhead

6
19
60

5 29 77
59 Red Wharf Bay
16 78
20 Valley
13 Beaumaris
8 33 Conw
Llangefni
10 63 Bangor
Llanfairpwll
38 Menai Bridge
70
Caernarfon Llanddeiniolen
53 57 15
Brynrefail 42 12
Llanberis Capel Curig

Blaenau Ffestiniog
7
26
49
11 66 79 Porthmadog
Criccieth Portmeirion
31 35
67 17 Talsarnau
44 48 Pwllheli Harlech
58 18
21 Abersoch Llanelltyd
Aberdaron 69 50 14
75 25
Uwch Mynydd 3 45
Barmouth 22
Penmaenpool 76

47
Tywyn 55
71

N

This map is an indication
of the general area
in which a featured
restaurant can be found.

Scale

Kilometres
0 1 2 3 4 5   10   15

0 1 2 3 4 5   10
Miles